the first true super star

Words by Norman C. Habel
Pictures by Jim Roberts

Concordia Publishing House

℗ A PURPLE PUZZLE TREE BOOK

COPYRIGHT © 1973
CONCORDIA PUBLISHING HOUSE,
ST. LOUIS, MISSOURI

MANUFACTURED IN THE
UNITED STATES OF AMERICA
ALL RIGHTS RESERVED
ISBN 0-570-06538-0

What if you saw a ball aglow
come flying fast or spinning low,
and blinking, beeping, "Come, let's go"?
What would you do? Tell me!
Would you climb inside its purple eye
and fly it far across the sky
to solve the mystery?

What if you saw a superstar,
A superdooper snooper star,
come swirling like a racing car?
What would you do? Tell me!
Would you ride inside a superjet
and chase it through a red sunset
to solve the mystery?

What if you lived long, long ago,
when camels traveled very slow
and that bright star came shining low?
What would you do? Tell me!
Would you ride astride a camel grand
and bump across the burning sand
to solve the mystery?

I mean, would you really?

Well, many, many years ago
some wondering wise old men
did just exactly that.
Those wondering, wise old men
lived far away in the East,
in a land of mysteries.

For years those wise men sat
and wondered and wondered
about the stars that filled the sky
and why they all were there.

Then one day a bright surprise
hit the heavens and filled the skies.

High in the sky
was a superstar,
spinning around
like a dancing clown
having a wonderful time.

Suddenly it stopped
and burned like a flame
just ahead of the wise men
and ready to lead the way.

Where did it want to go?
And why would anyone follow a star
that he had never seen
to a place he had never been?

Well, those wondering wise old men
took their grand old, grumpy camels
with all the food they could find
and started to follow that star,
wherever the thing might go.

And do you know,
that star went west,
straight across the desert
where only camels can go,
and even they don't like it.
For as they bump across the sand
they groan with a grumpy groan:
    GRUM GEEEERUMP
    GRUM GEEEERUMP.
    I'll make you feel
    every bump on my hump.

But the wise men didn't mind.
They followed their star
for miles and miles
until they reached Jerusalem,
where the great King Herod lived.
And he was as grumpy, my friend,
as a dozen camels, end to end.

The wise men said to themselves,
"This star is a sign from God
   that somewhere a king has been born.
   And since this is Jerusalem
   the child must be Herod's son."

So those tired, dusty, wise old men,
   who had traveled for weeks on the trail,
   went to see King Herod
   who laughed when he saw them coming.

"We want to see the newborn King,"
   the wise men proudly said.
"We've come from afar
   and followed His star
   right to this very palace."

King Herod stopped laughing
   and began to get grumpy.
   He called his own wise men
   and asked them if they knew
   the place where this new King
   was likely to be born.

"In Bethlehem," his wise men said,
"where once King David was born,
many years ago.
It's a little country town,
just a little way down the road."

King Herod became more grumpy,
for he was a jealous man,
and he didn't want to lose his throne
to any country kid.

So he told the wise old men:
'Go, find that newborn King
and tell me where He lives.
For I would like to show my love
and worship Him myself."

But grumpy Herod had a plan,
deep inside his heart,
to try and kill that Baby Boy
and tear His town apart.

The wise men mounted their camels again
and the star kept shining ahead,
lighting up the road to Bethlehem
where the promised King was born,
just as God's prophets had said.

Then, out of the blue
that bright star flew
around and around,
like a dancing clown
having a wonderful time,
until it hovered and shone
above a little stable.

There in a stall where cattle eat
a man and a woman sat
with a bright, new Baby Boy.
And I'm sure you know who they are.

That's right!
The man's name was Joseph,
and Mary was his wife.

The Boy was God's own Son,
whom God had sent to earth,
along with one bright star
to celebrate His birth.

The wise men gave the Baby Jesus
the precious gifts they brought along
to honor their bright new King.
Some gifts were made of gold
that gleamed by the light of the star.
Some gifts were like perfume
that makes the air feel soft.
And some like a precious oil
that soothes your hands and face.

And you, what kind of gifts
would you like to bring
to Jesus Christ,
the newborn King?

When the wise men had to leave,
an angel whispered in their ear,
"Don't tell King Herod what you found,
or he'll try to kill the Boy."

So the wise men traveled home
along a different trail,
and that made Herod mad,
grumpy jealous mad,
for he wanted to kill the Child.

Then in a dream that Joseph had
an angel spoke to him:
"Go far away to Egypt
and far away from Herod,
where the Baby will be safe."

Mary, and Joseph, and Jesus
went all the way to Egypt,
and the wise men rode back home,
as the camels groaned their grumpy groan,
　　GRUM GEEEERUMP
　　GRUM GEEEERUMP.
　　I'll make you feel
　　every bump on my hump.

But the wise men didn't care,
for they had seen God's Son,
He was greater by far than any star,
and they knew that He would be
the answer to the Purple Puzzle mystery.

OTHER TITLES

SET I

WHEN GOD WAS ALL ALONE 56-1200
WHEN THE FIRST MAN CAME 56-1201
IN THE ENCHANTED GARDEN 56-1202
WHEN THE PURPLE WATERS CAME AGAIN 56-1203
IN THE LAND OF THE GREAT WHITE CASTLE 56-1204
WHEN LAUGHING BOY WAS BORN 56-1205
SET I LP RECORD 79-2200
SET I GIFT BOX (6 BOOKS, 1 RECORD) 56-1206

SET II

HOW TRICKY JACOB WAS TRICKED 56-1207
WHEN JACOB BURIED HIS TREASURE 56-1208
WHEN GOD TOLD US HIS NAME 56-1209
IS THAT GOD AT THE DOOR? 56-1210
IN THE MIDDLE OF A WILD CHASE 56-1211
THIS OLD MAN CALLED MOSES 56-1212
SET II LP RECORD 79-2201
SET II GIFT BOX (6 BOOKS, 1 RECORD) 56-1213

SET III

THE TROUBLE WITH TICKLE THE TIGER 56-1218
AT THE BATTLE OF JERICHO! HO! HO! 56-1219
GOD IS NOT A JACK-IN-A-BOX 56-1220
A LITTLE BOY WHO HAD A LITTLE FLING 56-1221
THE KING WHO WAS A CLOWN 56-1222
SING A SONG OF SOLOMON 56-1223
SET III LP RECORD 79-2202
SET III GIFT BOX (6 BOOKS, 1 RECORD) 56-1224

SET IV

ELIJAH AND THE BULL-GOD BAAL 56-1225
LONELY ELIJAH AND THE LITTLE PEOPLE 56-1226
WHEN ISAIAH SAW THE SIZZLING SERAPHIM 56-1227
A VOYAGE TO THE BOTTOM OF THE SEA 56-1228
WHEN JEREMIAH LEARNED A SECRET 56-1229
THE CLUMSY ANGEL AND THE NEW KING 56-1230
SET IV LP RECORD 79-2203
SET IV GIFT BOX (6 BOOKS, 1 RECORD) 56-1231

SET V

THE FIRST TRUE SUPER STAR 56-1242
A WILD YOUNG MAN CALLED JOHN 56-1243
THE DIRTY DEVIL AND THE CARPENTERS BOY 56-1244
WHEN JESUS DID HIS MIRACLES OF LOVE 56-1245
WHEN JESUS TOLD HIS PARABLES 56-1246
OLD ROCK THE FISHERMAN 56-1247
SET V LP RECORD 79-2204
SET V GIFT BOX 56-1248

SET VI

WONDER BREAD FROM A BOY'S LUNCH 56-1249
WHEN JESUS RODE IN THE PURPLE PUZZLE
    PARADE 56-1250
    WHEN JESUS' FRIENDS BETRAYED HIM 56-1251
    THE DEEP DARK DAY WHEN JESUS DIED 56-1252
    DANCE, LITTLE ALLELU, WITH ME 56-1253
    THE KEY TO THE PURPLE PUZZLE TREE 56-1254
    SET VI LP RECORD 79-2205
    SET VI GIFT BOX 56-1255

the PURPLE PUZZLE TREE